READ AND SHARE®

Bible

D1372290

For:

Ivy

From:

Grandma Harer

Date:

9-7-12

READ AND SHARE®
Early Reader
Bible
Stories

Bible Stories Retold by
Gwen Ellis

Illustrated by Steve Smallman

A Division of Thomas Nelson Publishers

NASHVILLE   DALLAS   MEXICO CITY   RIO DE JANEIRO

Published in Nashville, Tennessee, by Tommy Nelson in association with Lion Hudson plc. Tommy Nelson is a registered trademark of Thomas Nelson, Inc.

Stories based on *The Holy Bible, International Children's Bible*®, copyright © 1986, 1988, 1999, 2005 by Thomas Nelson, Inc.

Stories retold by Gwen Ellis
Illustrated by Steve Smallman

Thomas Nelson titles may be purchased in bulk for educational, business, fund-raising, or sales promotional use. For information, please e-mail SpecialMarkets@ThomasNelson.com.

ISBN 978-1-4003-8875-2 (SE)

Library of Congress Cataloging-in-Publication Data

Ellis, Gwen.
  Read and share Bible : more than 200 best-loved Bible stories / by Gwen Ellis.
    p. cm.
  ISBN: 978-1-4003-0853-8 (hardback)
  1. Bible stories, English. I. Title.
BS551.3.E55 2007
220.9'505—dc22

2006029401

Worldwide co-edition produced by
Lion Hudson plc,
Mayfield House, 256 Banbury Road,
Oxford OX2 7DH, England
Telephone: +44 (0) 1865 302750
Fax: +44 (0) 1865 302757
Email: coed@lionhudson.com
www.lionhudson.com

12 13 14 15 16 MCP 5 4 3 2 1

Give thanks to the Lord and pray to him.
Tell the nations what he has done.
Sing to him. Sing praises to him.
Tell all the wonderful things he has done.
Be glad that you are his.
Let those who ask the Lord for help be happy.
Depend on the Lord and his strength.
Always go to him for help.
Remember the wonderful things he has done.
Remember his miracles and his decisions. . . .
He will keep his promises always.

PSALM 105:1–5, 8

Dear Parents

What you are holding in your hands is not just a book; it's a unique way to share God's Word with the children in your life, a way to help them come to know God's love, goodness, and faithfulness to us . . . and to share that good news with others.

In today's fast-paced world, it's not easy to carve out special times together with family. But it's my hope that the bite-size stories in this book will enable you to make the most out of those important times together.

As I selected the stories for *Read and Share® Bible*, I decided to include, not only well-known Bible stories, but also some that rarely appear in Bible storybooks. They, too, are significant in understanding God's love. The stories are also in chronological order to show children how the whole Bible fits together. Based on *The Holy Bible, International Children's Bible®*, each story has a Scripture reference to make it easy for you to read more about the story from the Bible. (Check out the tips on the following page for more helpful ways to use this book.)

God bless you and the children in your life as together you get to know Him better through the pages of this book.

Blessings,
Gwen Ellis

Tips on How to Use This Book

* Read these stories aloud to your children. Dramatize the story as you read. Make the wind *whoosh* and the thunder *boom*. The kids will love it, listen, respond, and remember. Older children will benefit from reading the story independently in addition to hearing it read aloud.

* When the story is over, discuss the questions, thoughts, and extra information in the boxes at the end of the stories. These sharing and discussion prompts make this Bible storybook unique, and they help the child to focus on the real meanings of the stories. Don't miss out on this important feature.

* Use the book as a tool to help refresh your memory of favorite stories. You may even hear one you haven't heard before. Either way, embrace it as a learning experience for both you and your child.

* Use *Read and Share® Bible* stories as part of a family Bible study, in Sunday school classes, for bedtime, or for any other special reading time with children.

Contents

New Testament Stories — 1

Jesus Is Born
The Angel's Message	Luke 1:5–20	2
A Baby Named John	Luke 1:57–66	4
Mary's Big Surprise	Luke 1:26–38	6
Joseph Marries Mary	Matthew 1:18–25	8
God's Baby Son	Luke 2:1–7	10
Some Sleepy Shepherds	Luke 2:8–12	12
What the Shepherds Saw	Luke 2:13–20	14
Gifts for Baby Jesus	Matthew 2:1–12	16
Another Journey	Matthew 2:13–15	18
Home at Last!	Matthew 2:19–23	20

The Boy Jesus
Where Is Jesus?	Luke 2:41–45	22
Jesus with the Temple Teachers	Luke 2:46–50	24

John the Baptist
The Man Who Ate Locusts	Matthew 3:1–13; Mark 1:4–9	26
John Baptizes Jesus	Matthew 3:13–17	28

Jesus' Life
Jesus Tempted by Satan	Matthew 4:1–4	30
On Top of the Temple	Matthew 4:5–7	32
The Kingdoms of the World	Matthew 4:8–11	34
Jesus Heals a Sick Boy	John 4:46–51	36
Jesus Brings a Girl Back to Life	Mark 5:22–43	38
A Little Boy Helps Jesus	John 6:1–13	40

Jesus Walks on the Water	Mark 6:45–53	42
Jesus Loves Children	Luke 18:15–17	44
A Very Short Man	Luke 19:1–10	46
A Coin in a Fish	Matthew 17:24–27	48
A Blind Man Sees Again	Mark 10:46–52	50
A Very Poor Woman	Mark 12:41–44	52
Jesus Stops a Storm	Mark 4:35–41	54
One Lost Sheep	Luke 15:3–7	56
A Son Spends All His Money	Luke 15:11–13	58
The Man Who Ate Pig Food	Luke 15:14–19	60
Going Home to Father	Luke 15:20–32	62
Jesus' Best Friends	Luke 10:38–42	64
Jesus Brings Lazarus Back to Life	John 11:1–44	66
One Man Says Thank You	Luke 17:11–19	68

Jesus' Death and Resurrection
Jesus Borrows a Donkey	Luke 19:28–35	70
Jesus Rides Like a King	Luke 19:36–38; John 12:12–16	72
Jesus Shows How to Serve	John 13:1–17	74
The First Lord's Supper	Matthew 26:26–29; 1 Corinthians 11:23–25	76

Jesus Prays for Help	Matthew 26:36–40;	
	Mark 14:32–42; Luke 22:39–46	78
Jesus Is Arrested	Matthew 26:45–56;	
	Luke 22:45–51; John 18:10–11	80
Pilate Questions Jesus	Luke 22:52–23:25	82
Jesus Is Killed on a Cross	Matthew 27:27–40;	
	Mark 15:25–27	84
A Dark Day	Matthew 27:45–54;	
	Luke 23:44–49; Hebrews 9	86
Jesus Is Laid in a Tomb	Luke 23:50–56	88
A Big Surprise	Matthew 28:1–10	90
Jesus Is Alive!	Matthew 28:5–8; Luke 24:9–12	92
Jesus Eats Dinner with Two Friends	Luke 24:13–32	94
Jesus Appears to a Room Full of Friends	Luke 24:33–49	96
Jesus Goes to Heaven	Luke 24:50–53; Acts 1:6–11	98
The Holy Spirit Comes		
God's Spirit Comes to Help	Acts 2:1–4	100
Everyone Hears and Understands	Acts 2:5–42	102

A Beggar at the Temple   Acts 2:43–3:10   104
Philip Meets an Ethiopian   Acts 8:26–31   106
Philip Baptizes
     the Ethiopian   Acts 8:32–40   108

Saul Becomes Paul
     A Mean Man   Acts 9:1–4   110
     Saul Is Blinded   Acts 9:4–9   112
     Ananias Helps Saul   Acts 9:10–18; 13:9   114

Peter
     Peter in Jail   Acts 12:1–18   116

Paul's Travels
     A Woman Who Sold
       Purple Cloth   Acts 16:12–15   118
     Earthquake!   Acts 16:16–36   120
     Some People Laugh
       at Paul   Acts 17:16–34   122
     Shipwrecked!   Acts 27   124
     A Poisonous Snake   Acts 28:1–6   126

The Best Is Yet to Come
     New Heaven and Earth   Revelation 21   128
     A Promise to All
       God's Children   1 Corinthians 2:9   130

New
Testament

An Angel's Message

Luke 1:5–20

A priest named Zachariah went to God's house to burn an incense offering. As soon as he was inside, the angel Gabriel appeared. "Zachariah, you and your wife, Elizabeth, will have a son. You will name him John," Gabriel said.

Zachariah didn't believe it was possible for Elizabeth and him to have a son. They were too old. "Because you don't believe me, Zachariah, you will not be able to talk until the baby is born," Gabriel said.

John was going to be a very important person. He would tell others to get ready because Jesus was coming.

A Baby Named John

Luke 1:57–66

Just as the angel Gabriel had said, a baby boy was born to Zachariah and his wife, Elizabeth.

Their friends were very happy for them. "Name him Zachariah after his father," they said. Zachariah still couldn't talk, so he wrote down, "His name is John." As soon as Zachariah wrote that, he could talk again.

His name is John.

People don't get to see angels very often, but when they do, they need to pay attention. Angels bring messages from God. What is another way God sends messages?

Mary's Big Surprise

Luke 1:26–38

Not long after his visit to Zachariah, the angel Gabriel went to see a young woman named Mary. She was a cousin to Elizabeth, Zachariah's wife. Mary lived in Nazareth and was engaged to marry Joseph, the carpenter.

"Don't be afraid, Mary," the angel said. "God is pleased with you. You will have a baby and will name Him Jesus. He will be called the Son of God." This was a big surprise to Mary.

What would you do if an angel suddenly appeared right here in front of you?

Joseph Marries Mary

Matthew 1:18–25

When Joseph heard the news that Mary was going to have a baby, he didn't know what to think. He wasn't married to her yet. God loved Joseph and wanted him to understand that the baby was from God and everything was going to be all right.

So God sent an angel to talk to Joseph in a dream. This angel told Joseph, "Name the baby Jesus. He will save people from their sins." When Joseph heard God's plan, he married Mary.

The name *Jesus* means "savior."
What does a savior do?

God's Baby Son

Luke 2:1–7

The ruler of the land, Augustus Caesar, made a new law to count all the people. Everyone had to register in their hometown. So Joseph and Mary went to their hometown, Bethlehem. The town was full of people. There was no place for Mary and Joseph to sleep.

Finally, Joseph found a place for them where the animals were kept. And that's where God's Baby Son was born. His first bed was on the hay in the box where the animals were fed.

Why do you think God would want His Son to be born where the animals were kept?

Some Sleepy Shepherds

Luke 2:8–12

That night, out in the fields, sleepy shepherds were taking care of their sheep. Suddenly an angel appeared in the sky. The angel's light was so bright, it hurt their eyes.

"Don't be afraid," the angel said. "I have good news for you. A baby was born in Bethlehem town tonight. He is your Savior. You will find Him lying in a feeding box."

Who was the first to hear about Baby Jesus?

What the Shepherds Saw

Luke 2:13–20

Then the whole sky filled up with so many angels no one could count them all. They sang, "Glory to God in heaven!" And then, when the song was over, the angels disappeared.

14

The shepherds hurried to Bethlehem. They found Mary and Joseph and saw Baby Jesus lying in the hay in the feeding box. The shepherds told them everything the angels had said about the child.

If you had been out there on the hill with the shepherds, what would you have been thinking when the angels left?

Gifts for Baby Jesus

Matthew 2:1–12

Soon many of the people who came to register in Bethlehem went home. Mary and Joseph moved into a house.

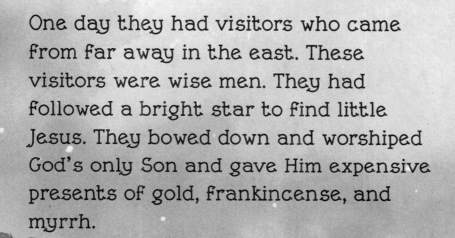

One day they had visitors who came from far away in the east. These visitors were wise men. They had followed a bright star to find little Jesus. They bowed down and worshiped God's only Son and gave Him expensive presents of gold, frankincense, and myrrh.

17

Why do you think the wise men came to see little Jesus?

Another Journey

Matthew 2:13–15

After the wise men left, God sent another angel to Joseph in a dream. "Take the child and Mary and go to Egypt," the angel said. "King Herod wants to kill Jesus. Stay in Egypt until I tell you it's safe to come home."

It was still night, but Joseph got up out of bed and took Mary and Jesus and headed for Egypt.

Joseph obeyed God immediately. And God kept his family safe. Why is it good to obey quickly?

Home at Last!

Matthew 2:19-23

Mary, Joseph, and Jesus stayed in Egypt until God sent another angel to Joseph in a dream. "Get up and take Mary and Jesus and go home," said the angel. King Herod had died. He could never hurt them again. God and His angels had kept Mary, Joseph, and Jesus safe.

So with happy hearts, they went home
to live in Nazareth.

**Whew! It was finally safe to go home. How do
you think Mary and Joseph felt about that?**

Where Is Jesus?

Luke 2:41–45

Every year Jesus' parents went to Jerusalem to celebrate the Passover. When Jesus was 12, they went as usual. When Mary and Joseph started home, they didn't see Jesus, but it was okay. They thought Jesus was traveling with friends.

Late in the day they realized He wasn't with any of their friends. Mary and Joseph were very worried and hurried back to Jerusalem, looking for Him all along the way. They were afraid they had lost Jesus.

What are some places where Mary and Joseph might have looked for Jesus?

Jesus with the Temple Teachers

Luke 2:46–50

When Mary and Joseph found Jesus, He was in the Temple—a place where God's people went to worship. Twelve-year-old Jesus was talking with some teachers just like He was one of them. He asked them questions, and He answered theirs.

His mother had a question too. "Son, why did You stay behind? We were worried about You." Jesus said, "You should have known I must be where My Father's work is!"

25

The Man Who Ate Locusts

Matthew 3:1–13; Mark 1:4–9

Jesus' cousin, John, became a preacher when he grew up. He lived in the desert and wore rough clothes and ate locusts and honey. (Locusts were like grasshoppers.) John told the people to change their hearts and lives and ask forgiveness for their wrongs because Jesus was coming soon.

One day when Jesus was grown up, too, He came to the place where John was preaching and baptizing people. Jesus asked John to baptize Him in the river.

When Jesus asked John to baptize Him, do you think John did it?

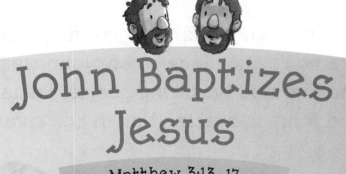

John Baptizes Jesus

Matthew 3:13–17

At first John didn't want to baptize Jesus. He thought Jesus should be the one to baptize *him*. But when Jesus said it needed to be this way, John obeyed and took Jesus into the river and baptized Him.

As Jesus came up out of the water,
God's Spirit, like a dove, came down to
Him from heaven. God spoke and said,
"This is My Son, and I love Him. I am very
pleased with Him."

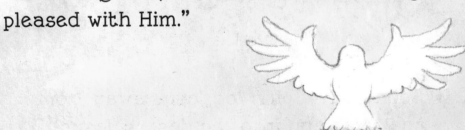

**Jesus set a good example for us by following
God's command to be baptized. Have you
been baptized?**

Jesus Tempted by Satan

Matthew 4:1–4

Soon God's Spirit led Jesus away from the river and into the desert. Jesus wanted to pray and think about what God wanted Him to do next. Jesus fasted—that means He didn't eat, so He got very hungry. Then the devil, Satan, appeared. Satan knew that Jesus was tired and hungry.

"Turn these rocks into bread," Satan told Jesus. Jesus knew that Satan was trying to get Him to do something wrong. Jesus had studied God's Word, so He remembered what He had learned from the Scriptures. He said, "A person does not live only by eating bread. A person lives by doing everything the Lord says."

Satan doesn't stop picking on people with just one try. He was not through with Jesus yet. Keep reading to see what happened next.

On Top of the Temple

Matthew 4:5-7

Satan took Jesus to Jerusalem and stood Him on the very top of the Temple. The Temple is where God's people worshiped. "If you are God's Son, jump down from this high place," Satan said. "It is written in the Scriptures that God's angels will catch You." That was not a smart thing for Satan to suggest, and Jesus knew it. He answered by saying, "It is also written in the Scriptures, 'Do not test God.'"

It is foolish to test or tease God. Testing God means doing very risky things that might get you hurt.

The Kingdoms of the World

Matthew 4:8–11

That sneaky devil, Satan, had one more test up his sleeve. He took Jesus to a high mountain and showed Him all the kingdoms of the world. Satan said, "Bow down and give honor to me, and I will give You all these things."

Jesus had an answer ready, "Go away from Me! It is written in the Scriptures, 'You must worship only the Lord God.'" So Satan went away.

Even though we can't see Satan, he tries to get us to do things that are wrong. What are some of the things Satan tries to get us to do?

Jesus Heals a Sick Boy

John 4:46–51

Jesus loved little children, and whenever He could, He helped them. One day an important man begged Jesus to come to his house and heal his sick son. But Jesus didn't go. Instead He said, "Go home. Your son will live."

36

The man believed Jesus and went home, but before he got there his servants met him and said, "Your son is well."

When we believe and trust someone to do something we cannot see, that is called *faith*. The man in this story trusted Jesus to keep a promise. Whom do you trust?

37

Jesus Brings a Girl Back to Life

Mark 5:22–43

Jesus also helped a little girl. Her father's name was Jairus, and he was an important man. "My little daughter is dying," Jairus said. "Please come and pray for her so she will get well and live." Before Jesus could go to the little girl, she died. But Jesus went anyway. With the child's mother and father and three of His followers, Jesus went in the girl's room and took her hand in His. "Little girl," Jesus said, "stand up!" And she did. She was well.

When we ask God for something, sometimes He says yes, and sometimes He says no. The most important thing is that He always hears us.

A Little Boy Helps Jesus

John 6:1–13

Great crowds of people followed Jesus to see His miracles and hear Him teach about God's love for them. The people sometimes forgot to take food with them. One day a huge crowd of 5,000 men and their families followed Jesus. It was late in the day when they reached Jesus, and the people were getting hungry.

The only one with any food was a little boy with five small loaves of bread and two fish. Jesus blessed the food. His closest followers and helpers gave it to the people. After everyone had plenty to eat, the helpers gathered up 12 baskets of leftover food.

41

What do you have that you could give Jesus? An offering? Some time to help someone?

Jesus Walks on the Water

Mark 6:45–53

Later that day Jesus told the followers who were His helpers to go to another city across the lake. He would come after a while. The helpers got into a boat. But that night in the middle of the lake, a strong wind came up. And the men had to work very hard to row the boat.

Then they saw something that frightened them more than the storm. They thought it was a ghost. But it wasn't a ghost. It was Jesus walking on the water. Jesus called to His helpers, "Don't be afraid." Then Jesus got into the boat, and the wind became calm.

If you had been in that boat,
what would you have done?

Jesus Loves Children

Luke 18:15–17

Many people wanted to see Jesus. When Jesus saw how sick and sad they were, He wanted to help them. One day some people brought their children to Him. His helpers tried to send them away. Jesus said, "Let the little children come to Me. Don't stop them. You must love and accept God like a little child if you want to enter heaven."

44

45

**If you were one of the children who got to sit
on Jesus' lap, what would you say to Him?**

A Very Short Man

Luke 19:1–10

Everywhere Jesus went,
there were crowds of people.
In one crowd there was a very
short man named Zacchaeus.
He wanted to see Jesus, but he
couldn't see over the crowd.
So he climbed a tree.

Jesus said, "Zacchaeus, come down so we can go to your house today." Zacchaeus hurried down and took Jesus to his home. Zacchaeus wanted to do good things. He told Jesus that he'd give half of his money to the poor.

Wouldn't it be exciting to have Jesus come to your house? What would you do if Jesus came to see you?

A Coin in a Fish

Matthew 17:24–27

Peter, one of Jesus' helpers, came to tell Jesus it was time for Him to pay taxes. But Jesus and Peter didn't have any money. Jesus knew just what to do. Jesus told Peter, "Go to the lake and catch a fish. You will find a coin in its mouth. Use that coin to pay our taxes."

Aren't you glad Jesus always knows the best thing to do? Talk to Him about your problems.

A Blind Man Sees Again

Mark 10:46–52

Sick people followed Jesus everywhere. They wanted Him to heal them. One man who was blind heard that Jesus was walking by. He cried out, "Jesus, please help me!" People told the man to be quiet, but Jesus asked the man, "What would you like Me to do for you?"

The man said, "I want to see again." So Jesus healed the man's eyes. How happy the man was to see again!

Do you know someone who is sick? You could pray right now and ask Jesus to make them well.

A Very Poor Woman

Mark 12:41-44

Jesus was watching people put their money into the collection box at the Temple where God's people worshiped. Some rich people were very proud as they put in a lot of money.

52

Then a very poor woman came. In went her two small coins. *Plunk! Plunk!* Jesus told His closest followers, "This woman gave more than the rich people with many coins. The rich people gave only what they did not need, but this poor woman gave all the money she had."

Why do you think the woman gave God all the money she had?

Jesus Stops a Storm

Mark 4:35–41

Jesus and His followers got into a boat and set out across the lake. Jesus was so tired that He fell asleep. Soon a strong wind began to blow. Waves came over the side of the boat. Everyone was very frightened.

They woke Jesus. "Help us, or we'll drown!" Jesus commanded the wind and waves to be still. The wind stopped, and there were no more waves coming into the boat. The lake became calm.

When you are frightened, what do you do?
Remember, Jesus is always there with you.
Just ask Him to help you. He will.

One Lost Sheep

Luke 15:3–7

Here is a story Jesus told. A man had 100 sheep, but he lost one. Now, what was he going to do? He left his 99 sheep safe at home and went looking for the one lost sheep.

He searched everywhere, and when he finally found the lost sheep, he was so happy. He put the sheep on his shoulders and carried it home.

How is Jesus like that shepherd looking for his one lost sheep? Remember, you are as important to Jesus as that one lost sheep was to the shepherd.

A Son Spends All His Money

Luke 15:11–13

Jesus told another story. A man had two sons. The younger son said, "Give me my share of the property and money." So the father divided the property and money between his younger son and older son.

The younger man went to another country far away. He had lots of fun spending every bit of his money.

Do you think the younger son was making a good decision? How do you think his father felt?

The Man Who Ate Pig Food

Luke 15:14–19

After the younger son's money was gone, he got very hungry. A man gave him a job feeding pigs. As the son fed the pigs, he was so hungry that he ate the pig food.

After a while he began to realize he had been very foolish. He said to himself, "My father's servants have plenty of food. I'm going home. I'll tell my father that I have done wrong. I'll ask him if I can just be a servant."

Wow, what a mess! What were some of the choices the son made that got him into a pigpen?

Going Home to Father

Luke 15:20-32

The younger son went home. He was worried that his father wouldn't want him. But his father had been looking for him every day for a long time.

When he saw his son, the father ran to meet him. He hugged him and gave him new clothes. He had a party to welcome him home. He told everyone, "My son was lost, but now he is found!"

The father in this story is like God. God sees us make bad choices, and He is sad. But He is always waiting for us to come back to Him.

Jesus' Best Friends

Luke 10:38–42

One day Jesus went to visit some best friends named Mary, Martha, and Lazarus. Martha was busy getting the meal ready. Mary was sitting and listening to Jesus talk.

Martha became angry and complained, "Jesus, don't You care that Mary left me to do all this work alone? Tell her to help me." Jesus said, "What Mary is learning from Me can never be taken away from her."

Why was Martha angry? What did Jesus tell her?

Jesus Brings Lazarus Back to Life

John 11:1-44

One day Lazarus got very sick. Mary and Martha sent a message to Jesus asking Him to come heal their brother. Even though Jesus loved His three friends, He waited two days to start the trip to see them, and Lazarus died before Jesus got there.

Martha and Mary said, "If You had come earlier, our brother wouldn't have died." Jesus was so sad He cried. Then He went to the tomb of Lazarus. He said, "Lazarus, come out!" And out came Lazarus, wrapped in the burial cloths. He was alive and well!

Sometimes when we ask Jesus for something, we have to wait—sometimes for a long time.

One Man Says Thank You

Luke 17:11–19

Ten men met Jesus as He was walking
along a road. They didn't come close
to Jesus because they had the horrible
skin disease, leprosy. They called out,
"Please help us!" Jesus told them they
were healed and sent them on their way.

As the men went on their way, the leprosy disappeared. Only one man came back. He bowed down to Jesus and thanked Him for what He had done.

We should remember to say thank you for what God has done for us. What has God done for you?

Jesus Borrows a Donkey

Luke 19:28–35

The first Passover happened when God's people left Egypt long ago. After that, God's people celebrated the Passover every year. One year Jesus and His closest followers went to Jerusalem to celebrate the Passover.

Before they got there, Jesus said to His followers, "Go into town and find a young donkey colt. Untie it and bring it to Me. If anyone asks where you are taking it, say, 'The Master needs it.'" When the men got back with the donkey colt, they spread their coats on its back. Jesus climbed on the colt.

Why do you suppose Jesus needed that donkey colt?

Jesus Rides Like a King

Luke 19:36–38; John 12:12–16

The donkey started to clippity-clop through the town. People came running. They threw their coats down for the donkey to walk on. They took palm branches and waved them in the air. "Praise God!" they shouted.

72

Some of them remembered the Scriptures that said, "Your king is coming . . . sitting on the colt of a donkey."

Why do you suppose they laid their coats down
for the donkey to walk on?
Did they think Jesus was a king?

Jesus Shows How to Serve

John 13:1–17

Soon it was time for the Passover dinner. Jesus and His closest followers gathered in a big room. Jesus stood up, took off His coat, got some water in a wash bowl, and wrapped a towel around His waist.

Then He started washing His followers' feet. Jesus did this to teach His friends they were to serve one another.

Jesus was serving His followers to set a good example. What could you do to serve your brothers and sisters and parents?

The First Lord's Supper

Matthew 26:26–29; 1 Corinthians 11:23–25

While Jesus and His closest followers were eating the Passover dinner, Jesus took some bread and thanked God for it. He broke the bread apart and said, "Take this bread and eat it. Do this to remember Me."

Next He took a cup and said, "When you drink this juice of the grape, remember Me." Jesus knew this was His last meal with His followers because He was about to be killed. He wanted His followers to always remember Him.

Today in church we still eat bread and drink the juice of the grape to remember Jesus. We call this time of remembering *Communion* or *The Lord's Supper.*

Jesus Prays for Help

Matthew 26:36–40; Mark 14:32–42;
Luke 22:39–46

Jesus and His followers went straight from dinner to a quiet garden. Jesus wanted to pray and ask God to make Him strong for what was about to happen. He took three of His closest followers—Peter, James, and John—with him. Jesus asked them to wait and pray.

He went a little farther into the garden so that He could pray by Himself. It was very late, and the three men were very tired. They couldn't keep their eyes open to pray. Soon they were asleep. Jesus woke them twice, but they went back to sleep each time.

When we have tough things ahead of us, we need to pray and ask God to help us.

Jesus Is Arrested

Matthew 26:45–56; Luke 22:45–51; John 18:10–11

The third time Jesus woke His followers, He said, "We must go. Here comes the man who has turned against Me." Just then a big crowd carrying torches and clubs came into the garden. Judas, one of Jesus' followers, was with them. He kissed Jesus on the cheek. It was a signal to the guards to arrest Jesus.

Peter pulled out his sword and cut off the ear of one guard. Jesus told Peter to put the sword away. Then He healed the guard's ear.

You might think the crowd would let Jesus go after He healed the man's ear. Well, they didn't. They arrested Him and took Him away.

Pilate Questions Jesus

Luke 22:52–23:25

Lots of people loved Jesus, but there were many who didn't like Him at all. After Jesus was captured in the garden, He was taken to the house of the high priest, then to Pilate, the Roman governor of Judea.

All night the rulers asked Jesus if He was God's Son. They did not believe that He was. Finally Pilate said that he didn't think Jesus was guilty. But the people who hated Jesus kept yelling until Pilate decided that Jesus had to die on a cross.

Jesus told everyone that He was God's Son, and that made some people very angry. But even if they didn't believe it, He was still God's Son.

Jesus Is Killed on a Cross

Matthew 27:27–40; Mark 15:25–27

Pilate's soldiers took Jesus and put a crown of thorns on His head and made fun of Him. Then they led Jesus out of the city to a place called Golgotha to be killed on a cross.

At nine o'clock in the morning, the soldiers nailed Jesus to the cross. They also put two robbers beside Jesus, one on the right and one on the left.

The day God's Son died on the cross was a sad day.
But God had a wonderful plan.
Keep reading and you'll see what it was.

85

A Dark Day

Matthew 27:45–54; Luke 23:44–49;
Hebrews 9

While Jesus was on the cross, the land
became dark from noon until three
o'clock. Then Jesus died, and there was a
big earthquake.

When the earth shook, the thick curtain in the Temple between the Holy Place and the Most Holy Place ripped from top to bottom. Now people could see inside the Most Holy Place. Before, only the High Priest got to see inside. When the soldiers at the cross saw what happened when Jesus died, they knew He really was the Son of God!

Jesus died because He loved us. He died so that our sins could be forgiven. Let's tell Him right now that we love Him for what He did on the cross.

Jesus Is Laid in a Tomb

Luke 23:50-56

A rich man, named Joseph of Arimathea, had a new tomb where he had planned to be buried. He took Jesus' body from the cross and put it in his own empty tomb.

Joseph and Jesus' friends wrapped His body in strips of linen and laid it carefully in the tomb. Roman soldiers came to guard the tomb. They rolled a huge stone over the door and sealed it in a way that would show if anyone tried to move the stone.

Everyone thought that since Jesus was dead, they would never see Him again. They were in for a big surprise!

A Big Surprise

Matthew 28:1–10

The day after Jesus was buried was a holy day, so His friends had to stay home. Then very early on Sunday morning, the first day of the week, the women went back to the tomb. It was the third day since Jesus died.

When the women got there, they couldn't believe their eyes. The stone had been rolled away! An angel of God was sitting on the stone! The soldiers were so frightened they were like dead men.

How do you think those women at the tomb felt when they saw the angel?

Jesus Is Alive!

Matthew 28:5–8; Luke 24:9–12

The angel said, "Don't be afraid. Jesus is alive." Those women were as happy as they could be! They ran to find other friends of Jesus.

Some of Jesus' friends didn't believe what the women said. But everything the women said was true. Jesus was alive! He had risen from death.

How long is forever? Jesus promised He would come back to life . . . and He did. Jesus is alive today and will be forever.

Jesus Eats Dinner with Two Friends

Luke 24:13–32

Two of Jesus' friends were walking along the road, and Jesus joined them. These two people didn't know it was Jesus who was walking with them. But they liked talking with this man.

They invited Him to have dinner at their house. Jesus came, and while He was thanking God for the food, the friends realized the man was Jesus. Then Jesus disappeared.

After Jesus was raised from the dead, He could appear and disappear. What would you do if Jesus suddenly appeared here?

Jesus Appears to a Room Full of Friends

Luke 24:33–49

One night Jesus appeared in a room where many of His friends were gathered. He told them to tell their family and friends and neighbors and even strangers that He is alive.

He told them to share everything He had taught them. They were to tell the people in Jerusalem first, but then they were to tell people everywhere. Jesus told them to wait in Jerusalem until God sent them a special gift of power from heaven.

Whom do you know that would like to hear all about Jesus' love?

Jesus Goes to Heaven

Luke 24:50–53; Acts 1:6–11

Jesus led His followers a little way out of town. Jesus prayed for His followers, and while He was praying, He started to rise up into heaven. Then a cloud hid Him from His followers.

98

As everyone was standing there staring up into heaven, two angels appeared beside them and said, "Jesus has been taken away from you and into heaven. He will come back in the clouds, just like He went away."

99

Remember the gift that God was going to send? Keep reading and see what happened.

God's Spirit Comes to Help

Acts 2:1–4

After Jesus went back to heaven, His friends and helpers were praying together in a big room. Suddenly something amazing happened.

First it sounded as if a huge wind were blowing. Next flames of fire flickered over every person's head. Then God's Spirit came, and everyone began to speak in different languages. This was the gift from God that Jesus had promised His followers.

Jesus' friends were happy. God's Spirit had come to live with them and to help them.

Everyone Hears and Understands

Acts 2:5–42

The night that God's Spirit came to Jesus' followers, there were people from many countries in Jerusalem. These people spoke different languages.

When they heard Jesus' friends praying, they went to see what the noise was all about. They found Jesus' friends telling about the great things God had done.

But they were all surprised to hear it in their own language. "What does this mean?" they asked.

God's Holy Spirit still helps those who follow Jesus today.

A Beggar at the Temple

Acts 2:43–3:10

After that day when the Holy Spirit first came, Jesus' followers began to do many miracles, telling people about God's love and how Jesus had come to save them. One afternoon Peter and John went to the Temple. A man who couldn't walk sat there begging for money. Peter looked at him and said, "I don't have any money, but I do have something else I can give you: By the power of Jesus Christ from Nazareth— stand up and walk!" Up jumped the man. His feet and ankles were now strong.

Do you know someone who is sick? Now is a good time to pray and ask Jesus to help them.

Philip Meets an Ethiopian

Acts 8:26–31

Philip was another one of Jesus' followers. He was busy telling people about Jesus when an angel spoke to him. "Go out on the road," the angel said. Along came a very important man from Ethiopia riding in his chariot. He was reading from the book of Isaiah.

Philip ran alongside the chariot and said, "Do you understand what you are reading?" No, the man didn't understand. He stopped the chariot and invited Philip to ride in the chariot and explain what the book meant.

God looks for people, like Philip, who are ready to do what He asks.

Philip Baptizes the Ethiopian

Acts 8:32–40

Philip explained the Scripture passage the man was reading. It was all about Jesus. The man asked, "Why don't I get baptized?" The Ethiopian man believed in Jesus, and he wanted to be baptized.

So they stopped the chariot, and Philip baptized him. Then God needed Philip in another place, and *whoosh!* Just like that, Philip was gone.

When we do what God asks of us, we don't know what will happen next. We just need to be ready for whatever it is.

A Mean Man

Acts 9:1–4

There was a mean man chasing after
Jesus' followers. His name was Saul.
He was sure that everything he heard
about Jesus was wrong. He didn't believe
any of it. He was sure he was right. So
he hurt, and even killed, people who
believed in Jesus.

Well, God wanted Saul to work for Him. So one day when Saul was on a journey, God sent a bright flash of light. It was so bright, Saul fell to the ground.

Why do you think God wanted Saul to work for Him?

Saul Is Blinded

Acts 9:4–9

"Saul! Why are you doing things against Me?" a voice said from inside the light. "Who are you?" asked Saul. "I am Jesus. Now get up and go into the city."

When Saul stood up, he was blind. His friends had to lead him into the city. Saul wouldn't eat or drink anything for three days.

**What will happen to poor, blind Saul?
Do you think he is ready to listen to God?**

Ananias Helps Saul

Acts 9:10–18; 13:9

God sent a man named Ananias to find Saul and pray for him so that Saul could see again. Ananias was scared of Saul. But Ananias believed in Jesus and went anyway.

Ananias prayed for Saul, and Saul's sight came back. On that day, God changed Saul's heart to make him kind to those who believed in Jesus. Saul was also called Paul. Soon Paul began to tell others about Jesus too.

Did you know that Paul became one of the greatest preachers who ever lived?

Peter in Jail

Acts 12:1–18

One day mean King Herod threw Peter, one of Jesus' followers, in jail. The king had 16 soldiers guard Peter so he couldn't get away. That night an angel came into Peter's cell. "Hurry! Get up!" the angel said. "Follow me." Peter thought he must be dreaming . . . but he wasn't. The chains fell off his hands, and the angel led him past the guards. When they came to the iron gate of the prison, it swung open on its own, and Peter was free.

God is always stronger than anything that can happen to us. We have to trust that He will always do what's best for us.

A Woman Who Sold Purple Cloth

Acts 16:12–15

After Paul became a follower of Jesus, he went everywhere teaching people about Jesus. Many times there was no building where he could meet with friends. One day he and his friends were looking for a place to meet by the river when they saw a group of women.

118

One woman was Lydia. Her job was selling purple cloth. She loved God, but didn't know about Jesus. Paul told her all about Jesus, and Lydia believed that Jesus was God's Son. Lydia invited Paul and his friends to stay at her house.

Some of your friends probably want to know Jesus. They are just waiting for someone to tell them about Him. You could be the one who tells them.

Earthquake!

Acts 16:16–36

Some people didn't like what Paul was preaching about Jesus. So they caught Paul and his helper, Silas, and threw them in jail. The two men were beaten, and their feet were fastened tightly so they couldn't run away. That night, instead of complaining or crying, Paul and Silas prayed and sang songs to God.

Suddenly there was an earthquake, and the jail doors popped open. The jailer thought his prisoners had escaped. He knew if the prisoners had escaped, he would be in big trouble. Paul called to him, "We are all here!" When the jailer came to them, he asked, "What must I do to be saved?" Paul told him all about Jesus.

If you had been beaten, thrown in jail, and had your feet pinned down, what would you be doing?

Some People Laugh at Paul

Acts 17:16–34

Paul traveled to Athens in Greece to tell people about Jesus. In Athens, Paul saw an altar with writing that said, "TO A GOD WHO IS NOT KNOWN." Paul began to preach. He told the people about the God who made the whole world.

Paul said that God doesn't live in temples that men build, but in their hearts. He told them about Jesus coming back to life after being dead. Some of the people laughed at Paul, but some of the people believed in Jesus.

God wants all of us to tell others the Good News that Jesus is alive. Some people will believe, and some will laugh. We must pray for all of them.

Shipwrecked!

Acts 27

Paul got on a big ship. He was going to the city of Rome. The ship went very slowly because of strong winds blowing against it. Finally, the ship came to a safe harbor, and Paul told the captain he didn't think it was a good idea to leave the harbor for a while. But the captain disagreed, and he sailed anyway.

Soon a wind came up and blew hard on the ship. The sailors couldn't steer it. Paul knew they were in trouble—they might sink. He told the sailors to eat so they would be strong for the trouble ahead. Before long, the ship hit a sandbank and began to break into pieces. Everyone had to jump into the sea and swim for the beach. They all made it to shore safely.

How scary! A shipwreck! Where did they land? What happened next?

A Poisonous Snake

Acts 28:1–6

All the people from the shipwreck were now on the island of Malta, near the country of Greece. The people who lived on the island were very kind. They built a fire and invited the passengers to warm themselves.

Paul helped by gathering wood for the fire, and as he did, a poisonous snake bit him on the hand. Paul just shook the snake off into the fire. He was not even hurt. The island people waited for him to fall down dead from the poison, but Paul was just fine.

Why do you think Paul did not die when the poisonous snake bit him?

New Heaven and Earth

Revelation 21

One of the biggest promises God ever made was that we will live with Him in heaven forever. He said that there would be a new heaven and a new earth and we would get a new body—one that won't get old but will live forever.

In the new heaven, no one will ever be sad again. No one will ever die again. The streets will be made of gold, and there will be gates of pearl. Everything will be more beautiful than anything you can imagine. And best of all, Jesus will be there. We will be with Him forever.

What is the most beautiful thing you have ever seen? Heaven will be a thousand times more beautiful.

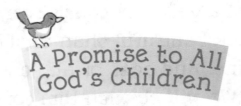

A Promise to All God's Children

"No one has ever seen this.
No one has ever heard about it.
No one has ever imagined
what God has prepared
for those who love him."

1 Corinthians 2:9